C000151709

GALORE PARK

So you really want to learn

Junior English

Book 3

Answer Book

Andrew Hammond MA

Series Editor: Susan Elkin MA BA(Hons) Cert Ed.

www.galorepark.co.uk

Published by Galore Park Publishing Ltd
19/21 Sayers Lane, Tenterden, Kent TN30 6BW
www.galorepark.co.uk

Text copyright Andrew Hammond © 2006

The right of Andrew Hammond to be identified as the author of this Work has been asserted by him in accordance with sections 77 and 78 of the Copyright, Designs and Patents Act 1988.

Typesetting by Typetechnique, London W1
Printed and bound by CPI, Antony Rowe, Chippenham

ISBN-13: 978 1 902984 85 8

All rights reserved: no part of this publication may be reproduced, stored in a retrieval system, or transmitted in any form or by any means, electronic, mechanical, photocopying, recording or otherwise, without either the prior written permission of the copyright owner or a licence permitting restricted copying issued by the Copyright Licensing Agency, 90 Tottenham Court Road, London W1P 0LP.

First published 2006, reprinted 2007, 2010

A pupil's book is available to accompany this book

ISBN-13: 978 1 902984 80 3

Details of other Galore Park publications are available at
www.galorepark.co.uk

ISEB Revision Guides, publications and examination papers
may also be obtained from Galore Park.

Contents

Introduction

The following book offers teachers and parents a range of recommended answers to the questions in *Junior English 3*.

In some cases an answer will be a definitive one – regurgitating literal information, writing a definition, or adding a prefix, for example – but there are many other instances when questions require more reflection and as a result, answers will vary. This is good practice, for English at this level is not an exact science. Children need to be encouraged to reflect, consider and express opinions in response to what they have read. For such questions, suggested answers are offered here, but they do not need to be taken too literally, or followed too rigidly. The beauty (and the frustration!) of language learning is that there may be an infinite range of acceptable answers out there. If the children have articulated their views coherently, and supported what they have said with some direct reference to the passage, they must be rewarded.

When working through the questions with your class or child, encourage them to see how the meaning of a word or phrase is always inextricably linked to the context in which it appears – i.e. the sentence that surrounds it. There are many questions that ask for translations, or definitions, of words and phrases. In these cases particularly, it is important to encourage young readers to 'go back to the text' and see how the author has used the word or phrase in the specific context. This is good preparation for Common Entrance, which requires careful, and repeated, reading of passages to ascertain meanings, draw inferences and deductions and reach conclusions. To this end, line references are given throughout *Junior English 3*.

Likewise, the old adage, 'read the question carefully' applies, and one might add 'read the answer' too, for mistakes are often missed in the rush to reach the end of a comprehension exercise. Above all, the children need to move beyond a cursory glance at passages and accompanying questions if they are to avoid those tangential answers that can be so costly in examinations.

Comprehension tasks are most effective when they encourage readers to *think* about what they are reading and *communicate* their relevant responses in efficient and enlightening ways. I hope that *Junior English 3* and this accompanying answer book assist you in encouraging children to become thoughtful, confident and communicative students.

Good luck.

AJH
March 2006

Chapter 1

Exercise 1.1

1.   The Billeting Officer has called at Tom Oakley's door to enquire if he is willing to look after an evacuee.

2.   The word harassed means 'tormented' or 'stressed'.

3.   Tom does not seem pleased to see his visitors. Words that show his displeasure include: bluntly (line 1), impatiently (line 28), abruptly (line 39) and harshly (line 50).

4.   Willie's mother requested that her son should be looked after by someone who is religious or lives near a church.

5.   Willie regards Tom as a large, overpowering man, with rough skin and a booming voice. (Quotes from the passage may include: 'a giant, with skin like coarse, wrinkled brown paper and a voice like thunder').

6.   Responses will vary, but the general theme should be: Tom is a strong and forceful character, ill-tempered and impatient, but the fact that he allows Willie to stay with him suggests that he has a good heart.

Exercise 1.2

1.   The children were evacuated from cities to the countryside to escape the dangers of German air raids.

2.   The three modes of transport are: train, bus and boat.

3.   Some evacuees returned home to their parents because they felt homesick.

4.   Trophies were pieces, or fragments, of bombs or crashed aircraft, found in amongst the rubble and debris left by a bombing raid.

5.   The scrap metal was taken to dumps, melted down and often used to make aircraft and weapons.

6.   Possible definitions are:
    (a) *evacuee*: a person sent away from home to a safer location, especially during a war
    (b) *rationed*: when the amount of food or other provisions a person is allowed is limited due to short supply
    (c) *homesick*: missing home

Exercise 1.4

1. The Billeting Officer arrived at Tom's door.
2. Can you look after an evacuee?
3. I've told you I can't!
4. The children looked tired and hungry.
5. What a sorry sight!
6. Have you travelled far?

Exercise 1.5

Nervously, Willie followed Tom into a dark hallway. It took a few seconds for his eyes to adjust from the brilliant sunshine he had left to the comparative darkness of the cottage. He could just make out the shapes of a few coats hanging on some wooden pegs and two pairs of boots standing below.

Exercise 1.6

1. She <u>gave</u> him an awkward smile.
2. She <u>paused</u> and <u>took</u> a deep breath.
3. The woman <u>touched</u> the boy at her side and <u>pushed</u> him forward.
4. Some children <u>gathered</u> scrap metal, such as old pots and pans.
5. Sweets <u>were rationed</u>, and there <u>were</u> fewer toys in the shops.

Exercise 1.7

1. <u>They</u> all looked bewildered and exhausted.
2. <u>Tom</u> gave a snort.
3. <u>Wartime</u> was very frightening and confusing.
4. <u>Many children</u> never left the cities.
5. But <u>town children</u> soon got used to playing among the ruined buildings and streets blocked with rubble.

Exercise 1.8

1. He noticed a <u>small boy</u> at her side.
2. She flushed slightly. (*no object*)
3. One tiny dark-haired girl in the front was cuddling <u>a new teddy bear</u>.
4. He glared at <u>Willie</u>.
5. The boy was thin and sickly-looking (*no object*)

Exercise 1.9

There are as many possible sentences as there are pupils, but some suggestions are:

1. The night was drawing in and the temperature was falling.
   The brave knight rode into battle on his white charger.
2. The young boy guessed the weight of the giant vegetable.
   The children were asked to wait quietly in the corridor.
3. Michael presented his mother with a pretty flower for her birthday.
   Flour is an essential ingredient for making bread.
4. The deer darted across the road, startling the drivers.
   Grandma said that her photo album was very dear to her.
5. The soldier was awarded a medal for her bravery.
   Jane was asked not to meddle with the video controls.

Exercise 1.10

1. would
2. (correct)
3. scene
4. peace
5. (correct)

Chapter 2

Exercise 2.1

1. The poem is written from a tree's point of view.
2. We rely on trees for: oxygen which they make; wood for furniture; loam for our gardens and for lighting fires (beacons and flares).
3. 'We flare to guide' refers to the trees being used to light fires to illuminate our way.
4. The speaker (a tree) may be threatened by Man if we chop more trees down than we plant (deforestation).
5. Possible definitions are:
    (a) *slake*: satisfy (a thirst)
    (b) *loam*: fertile soil
    (c) *revere*: respect; hold in high esteem
    (d) *beacon*: a fire or light, set up in a prominent position as a warning or guide
6. Answers will vary, but a suggested response is:
    By using the word green here, the poet is emphasising the idea that we are destroying living, live things. The phrase makes us feel sympathy for trees and encourages us to see them as living objects rather than just as firewood.

Exercise 2.2

1. The Yanomami people live in the Amazon rainforest, near the Brazil-Venezuela border.
2. A *yano* is a ring-shaped communal building that houses over a dozen families in the rainforest.
3. Answers must include any two of the following: food, medicines, wood and palm fronds to build the yano.
    (The questions asked for things that help the Yanomami *survive*, so cotton for aprons, dye for face make-up and flowers and shells for decorations may not be acceptable answers here.)
4. The urucu plant provides the red dye which they paint on their faces and bodies to make themselves look beautiful.
5. (a) Answers may vary, for example:
    Zeca learns by accompanying her mother on regular trips into the forest and to the riverside, where she is taught the skills she needs for life in the rainforest.

(b) Answers may vary, for example:

The skills include: knowing which wild fruit and berries are safe to eat; how to thread necklaces; where to find crabs and crayfish; and how to make bread from manioc.

6. Answers may vary upon the following theme:

Zeca's mother is worried because she fears that their forest home may be threatened by outsiders, bringing disease and destroying the trees.

7. Possible definitions are:

(a) *dye*: a natural or man-made substance used to colour something

(b) *adorn*: decorate

(c) *hammock*: a bed of canvas or other material, hung from two ends

(d) *foreigners*: people from another country

Exercise 2.4

2. collective
3. proper
4. compound
5. common
6. abstract

Exercise 2.5

1. The Yanomami people live in the rainforests of Brazil.
2. The Amazon rainforest of South America is the largest forest in the world.
3. It takes a long time to travel from Great Britain to South America.
4. Sometimes Zeca helps her mother with the weeding.
5. The country of Brazil shares a border with Venezuela.

Exercise 2.6

1. Zeca made aprons and <u>waistbands</u> for the other villagers.
2. Tom packed his <u>suitcase</u> and set off for South America.
3. Deep in the <u>rainforest</u>, the Yanomami people built their new yano.
4. Zeca found some beautiful shells along the <u>riverside</u>.
5. Tom peered out of the aeroplane window to see vast stretches of <u>woodland</u> below.

Exercise 2.7

1.   motorcycle
2.   afternoon
3.   clockwork
4.   hedgehog
5.   lighthouse
6.   bagpipes
7.   chatterbox
8.   blacksmith
9.   sweetheart
10.   grapefruit

Exercise 2.11

1.   funny / funnier / funniest
2.   coloured / colourful / colourless
3.   misty
4.   logical
5.   hopeful / hopeless
6.   rested / restful
7.   joyful / joyous
8.   loved / lovely / loving / loveless
9.   cynical
10.   dirty / dirtier / dirtiest

Exercise 2.12

2.   rain
3.   comic
4.   revenge
5.   cheese
6.   beast
7.   delight
8.   gust
9.   idiot
10.   interest

Chapter 3

Exercise 3.1

1. Granny reacts to Laura's news by smiling and patting her hand.
2. Mother sent Laura out to fetch back some limpets or anything else she could find.
3. Laura was unable to fish from the rocks because the sea was too rough.
4. The huge wave breaks over the ship's stern, causing it to keel over. It remains on its side, wallowing in the waves.
5. Everyone wanted to give up after the gig (rowing boat) which they were sailing in capsized, throwing everyone into the sea.
6. Alternative words include:
   (a) *driving*: blowing, lashing, whipping
   (b) *hauling*: dragging, hugging, pulling, towing, tugging
   (c) *icy*: cold, bitter, freezing, frosty, wintry

Exercise 3.2

1. The historic find is a five-metre-long piece of wood which could be the missing front stem from the keel of the Tudor warship, Mary Rose.
2. The divers had to endure murky waters to sift through mounds of silt, ten metres below the surface.
3. The team is particularly excited because it could mean that the final jigsaw piece of the Mary Rose has been found – the missing front section can now be put on the ship and displayed. The discovery may also lead to further treasures being found on the same site.
4. Answers will vary. Some suggestions are: Prince Charles is president of the Mary Rose Trust and so he has a personal interest in the warship; including the views of a senior member royal increases the article's appeal.
5. Possible definitions are:
   (a) *yielded*: produced; delivered; provided
   (b) *fortified*: equipped with defensive works to protect against attack
   (c) *optimist*: a person who is hopeful or confident about the future
   (d) *forerunner*: precursor; prototype; first version; something that precedes others

Exercise 3.4

1. 'There's men in the sea,' she said, 'We saw them from Samson Hill.'
2. 'Is it true?' cried Father. 'Have we got a wreck?'
3. 'Rushy Bay!' he shouted, confidently.
4. Chief executive of the Mary Rose Trust, John Lippiett, said, 'It is an extraordinary discovery.'
5. 'The story of the Mary Rose has intrigued generations of people,' said the Prince.

Exercise 3.5

1. 'Is it true?' cried Father, <u>anxiously</u>. 'Have we got a wreck?'
2. 'Hello, dear,' Granny May said <u>sweetly</u>.
3. 'Will you go and collect some limpets?' asked Mother, <u>politely</u>.
4. 'This could be the most important maritime archaeological find in England in the last 20 years,' he said <u>proudly</u>.
5. 'It's <u>hugely</u> exciting and <u>vitally</u> important,' she added <u>enthusiastically</u>.

Exercise 3.7

1. merry – merrily
2. peaceful – peacefully
3. warm – warmly
4. pathetic – pathetically
5. pleasing – pleasingly

Exercise 3.8

1. naughtily – naughty
2. confidently – confident
3. abruptly – abrupt
4. cheekily – cheeky
5. stoically – stoic / stoical

Chapter 4

Exercise 4.1

1.   The phrase that shows they are sitting in an orchard is 'There was still the sound of leaves'.
2.   Words will vary, but may include:
     empty; lonely; plain; hollow; unsettling; frightening; horrifying.
3.   Meg calls out to Charles either because she wants to help him or she wants him to help her – she does not know which.
4.   Possible answers should be on the following theme:
     By writing the sentence as a separate paragraph, the writer emphasizes Meg's desperate situation. The effect is that it makes her predicament seem even more dramatic, building tension and suspense for the reader.
5.   Meg describes her experience as a 'nightmare' because it feels unlike anything she has experienced whilst being awake, and it seems too frightening to be a regular dream.
6.   Possible definitions include:
     (a) *extinguished* : put out; stopped; put an end to
     (b) *fragment* : a piece or part broken off from something larger
     (c) *corporeal* : material; physical; tangible
     (d) *void* : empty space; vacuum; hole

Exercise 4.2

1.   The best way of checking that your watch is accurate is by listening to the Greenwich time signal on the radio (the BBC's 'pips').
2.   The astronomers at Greenwich checked the accuracy of their clocks by observing the position of the stars.
3.   The BBC's 'pips' are six short sounds played in succession on the radio, usually on the hour and at certain times during the day, to signal the exact time.
4.   Some of the earliest mechanical clocks, without faces or hands, told the time by striking each quarter hour.
5.   Answers may include:
     Keeping a close track of time may be more important to us today than it was many years ago because our lives are now more influenced by timetables, schedules, appointments and deadlines.

6.   Possible meanings are:
        (a) *transmission*: communication; presentation; airing (or a programme)
        (b) *succession*: following in order
        (c) *astronomer*: a person who studies the stars
        (d) *predict*: prophesy; make a statement about the future

Exercise 4.4

The astronomers at Greenwich <u>used</u> the stars to <u>check</u> the accuracy of their clocks. Each day the earth <u>spins</u> once on its axis, and because of this we <u>see</u> the sun seeming to <u>move</u> across the sky. It <u>rises</u> higher during the morning and <u>sinks</u> lower during the afternoon. The sun <u>is</u> only one of many stars which we <u>see</u> <u>moving</u> in this way. From their records, the astronomers <u>were</u> <u>able</u> to <u>predict</u> when each of the brightest stars <u>would</u> <u>reach</u> its highest point, and this <u>gave</u> them a reliable means of <u>checking</u> their clocks.

Exercise 4.6

1.   This morning I had English, French, Geography and Music.
2.   Will the following boys please report to my office: James, Santosh, Peter and Simon.
3.   At the greengrocer's shop I bought a cauliflower, some beans, a melon and a bag of potatoes.
4.   Since buying the motor-caravan, Grandpa and I have been to Somerset, Devon, Suffolk and North Yorkshire.
5.   On the menu today we have a choice of lasagna, shepherd's pie, curry or salmon.

Exercise 4.7

1.   Bravely, confidently and with no sign of wobbling, Molly rode her new bicycle.
2.   The dark, lonely and mysterious forest looked unwelcoming to the traveller.
3.   After a long day at work, Michael was looking forward to a long, hot and relaxing bath.
4.   The music examiner said the student had played confidently, accurately and with lots of feeling.
5.   The climb to the summit was painful, dangerous and very long.

Exercise 4.8

Verb	Past tense
to start	I started
to sing	I sang
to write	I wrote
to wish	I wished
to sweep	I swept
to look	I looked
to read	I read
to drive	I drove
to find	I found
to arrive	I arrived

Chapter 5

Exercise 5.1

1. Responses may vary. A suggested answer is:
    When the narrator says 'the forest stretched its fingers out to lash at your eyes' he is referring to the branches of the trees brushing your face as you pass by.
2. The silver light is coming from the moon.
3. Answers will vary but may include:
    On the night the narrator returns to the wood, he sees clawing tree branches, gnarled roots and splashes of moonlight on the forest floor. There is not a sound. The atmosphere of the forest is unwelcoming and frightening in places, causing him to run for the clearing.
4. The writer did not expect to find the Keeper in the goalmouth at that time as he thought he depended on daylight and would therefore not materialise at night.
5. Answers will vary but may include: a ghost; a ghoul; an angel; a deceased relative; a figment of the writer's own imagination.
6. Possible definitions include:
    (a) *canopy*: uppermost part of branches in a forest; an overhanging covering
    (b) *drenched*: thoroughly wet; soaked; saturated; covered completely
    (c) *materialise*: appear; become visible
    (d) *outraged*: annoyed; angry; fuming; irritated; mad

Exercise 5.2

1. The reason given for England losing their quarter-final match against West Germany is that they were without their first-choice goalkeeper, Gordon Banks.
2. Many England fans look back on this match as the 'real final' because England were the defending champions (holders of the Cup) and Brazil were the favourites to win it off them. Everyone expected them to face each other in the final.
3. Pele began celebrating before the ball had even reached the net.
4. Brazil won the match in the end.
5. Possible definitions are:
    (a) *majestically*: beautifully; impressively; grandly; regally
    (b) *epic*: grand; impressive; classic; heroic
    (c) *defining*: crucial; significant; decisive; important
    (d) *folklore*: traditional beliefs or customs of a community; legends; myths

Exercise 5.5

Answers will vary. Some suggestions are:

1. The player walked <u>off</u> the pitch.
2. The goalkeeper stood <u>behind</u> the goalpost.
3. 'We'll meet <u>after</u> the match for a drink.'
4. 'Walk <u>over</u> the bridge and you'll reach the stadium.'
5. The ball disappeared <u>into</u> the bushes.

Exercise 5.7

1. small – smaller, smallest
2. high – higher, highest
3. rich – richer, richest
4. keen – keener, keenest
5. bright – brighter, brightest

Exercise 5.8

Adjective	Comparative	Superlative
pretty	prettier	prettiest
beautiful	more beautiful	most beautiful
sunny	sunnier	sunniest
sad	sadder	saddest
gracious	more gracious	most gracious
busy	busier	busiest

good – better – best
many – more – most

Chapter 6

Exercise 6.1

1.   Daedalus had prepared for their escape by making wings from bird feathers and setting aside four balls of wax with which to fix them.
2.   Daedalus reminded his son that his wings were fixed with wax, which melts when warmed up. So he warned Icarus not to fly too close to the sun.
3.   The phrase 'snow-white' makes the wings seem even more beautiful and delicate, like snowflakes. (And snow melts quickly in the sun too, so it reminds us how dangerous the flight will be for Icarus and his father.)
4.   Answers will vary. Suitable alternatives include: shouted, exclaimed, hollered, yelled, roared, boasted.
5.   Icarus could almost believe that 'he had never been anything but a flying creature' because he was enjoying swooping and zooming so much, and was able to fly so successfully.
6.   The experience of Icarus shows us how important it is to listen carefully to the advice of others. When our parents tell us not to do something, it is always for our own good. It also reminds us that we are not invincible, and we must not become so carried away that we forget we might be in danger.

Exercise 6.2

1.   According to some people many years ago, in order to fly you needed to mimic the birds and their flapping wings, so they strapped wings to their arms and lunged into the air.
2.   These early attempts to fly were not successful. The people plummeted to the ground, often fatally.
3.   'Unlocking the secrets of flight' means finding out what we need to do to be able to fly like birds.
4.   Answers and diagrams will vary, but will need to include references to air flow, air pressure and their combined forces pushing and pulling on the wing.
5.   Possible definitions are:
     (a) *mythical*: imaginary; legendary; fabled
     (b) *mimic*: imitate; impersonate; take off; copy
     (c) *plummet*: fall or drop straight down; tumble; plunge
     (d) *pioneers*: developers of new ideas; explorers; innovators

Exercise 6.4

1. Daedalus (subject); strapped (verb)
2. Icarus (subject); ignored (verb)
3. The wax (subject); melted (verb)
4. Icarus (subject); plunged (verb)
5. Daedalus (subject); watched (verb)

Exercise 6.5

1. Daedalus and his son jumped off the balcony <u>and</u> began to fly.
2. The soldiers were after Daedalus and Icarus <u>but</u> they were able to escape.
3. Daedalus warned his son not to fly too high <u>but</u> he wouldn't listen.
4. Today you can fly in an aeroplane <u>or</u> you can take a ride in a hot air balloon.
5. Many people have tried to fly by strapping wings to their arms <u>but</u> no one has ever managed it.

Exercise 6.6

1. James said he would like to come <u>but</u> he may be a little late.
2. Gran knew who had eaten the cake <u>because/after</u> she saw the crumbs around my mouth.
3. The bride was late <u>because</u> the wedding car broke down.
4. The manager told his team <u>that</u> they could win the match if they really tried.
5. You had better avoid the prawns <u>unless</u> you want to have a stomach ache.

Exercise 6.8

Prefix	Greek word	Greek meaning	English words (answers may vary)
mega-	*megas*	great	megastore
micro-	*mikros*	small	microscopic
geo-	*ge*	earth	geology, geography
poly-	*polus*	much	polymath, polyphonic
octa-	*okto*	eight	octagon, octave

Exercise 6.9

Latin word	Meaning	English words (answers may vary)
habitare	*to live*	habitat, inhabitant
locus	*place*	location, local
multi	*many*	multiple, multiply
satis	*enough*	satisfied, satisfaction
quartus	*fourth*	quarter, quartet

Chapter 7

Exercise 7.1

1. The village is particularly dark at night time because it has no street lamps.
2. It is grease and oil left on the road from passing tractors that causes it to 'gleam greasily'.
3. (a) The 'spread fingers of trees' are branches that splay out like fingers on a hand.
   (b) Answers may vary. This metaphor has the effect of making the trees seem human, and to this extent more frightening because they may use their 'fingers' to reach out and grasp the narrator.
4. In the sixth stanza, after the speaker has mentioned the 'spirits' in the 'damp corner', he uses a series of short phrases, each one beginning with an imperative, advising the reader how to get out of the church as quickly as possible. Many of the lines of this stanza are shorter than others, which adds to the sense of urgency and panic.
5. I think the 'steel-blue miming of the little screen' is referring to a television, which cannot be heard from outside, so it seems like the characters on the screen are miming.

Exercise 7.2

1. The letter is actually selling a theatre production of *Midsummer Night's Dream*, which is touring schools. The writer is hoping the headmaster will want to pay for the theatre company to bring their show to the school, in return for £275.00.
2. This is not a traditional version, but a modern and abridged one.
3. The actors will also be offering the audience the opportunity to ask questions of the cast in a question and answer session which directly follows the play.
4. Members of the Rainbow Theatre Company believe that live theatre can bring the words of a script to life and create enthusiasm and interest in those who watch it.
5. Answers will vary, but may include any three of the following: exciting; new; great benefits; bring words to life; create interest and enthusiasm; talented; skilled actors and actresses; our rates are competitive.
6. Possible meanings are:
   (a) *abridged*: shortened; abbreviated; condensed
   (b) *benefits*: advantages; profits
   (c) *traditional*: of or relating to tradition; long-established; conventional; customary
   (d) *competitive*: relating to competition; as cheap as other companies' prices; attractively priced

Exercise 7.5

Answers will vary. Some suggestions follow.

1.   He looked back at the teacher with a blank face.
       He looked back at the teacher with a clueless expression on his face.
2.   The moon was a precious jewel.
       The moon resembled a gemstone, in appearance and value.
3.   By the second half, the team had a mountain to climb.
       By the second half, the team faced a big challenge.
4.   The examinations hung over the children's heads all term.
       The examinations were troubling the children throughout the term.
5.   The teacher had eyes in the back of her head.
       The teacher seemed able to notice what was going on behind her, even when she was facing the other way.

Exercise 7.6

Answers will vary. Some suggestions follow.

1.   She finished the race a nose in front.
2.   'Can you give me a hand?'
3.   It was time to face up to what she had done.
4.   With so much happening, Daniel was in danger of losing his head.
5.   Anna was looking very down in the mouth.

Chapter 8

Exercise 8.1

1. Toad has been accused of taking and driving away a motor car without the owner's consent (stealing it).
2. 'A person of means' means someone who has plenty of money at their disposal.
3. The cow is not in court. We know this because it says in the passage that Weasel Norman stands up and pretends to be a cow, saying 'I'm a cow. Moo.'
4. Answers will vary, but may include:
   I think the judge is open to bribery. He drops many hints to the prisoner, suggesting that he would be interested in favours: e.g. 'I keep thinking of that riverside mansion, where who knows I might one day be a guest...', 'Do you do kedgeree for breakfast at all?' and 'My inclination is to let the prisoner go free.'.
5. Toad does not accept his punishment without question. He is defiant.
6. Possible definitions are:
   (a) *clincher*: a fact or argument that settles a matter conclusively
   (b) *alleged*: claimed; suspected; supposed
   (c) *justice*: fairness; the administration of law and order
   (d) *conscience*: a sense of right and wrong; principles

Exercise 8.2

1. A new power unit makes the car feel lighter and more agile.
2. The Plus 8 came before the new Morgan Roadster.
3. The phrase 'redefines the Morgan driving experience' refers to the positive changes the new car makes to the way it feels to drive a Morgan.
4. The car is able to have such outstanding balance because of its 'low centre of gravity and near perfect weight distribution'.
5. (a) Answers may vary. I think this writing is aimed at potential customers who are considering buying a new Morgan. They may already be Morgan drivers, or new to the company.
   (b) The purpose of this writing is to persuade readers to buy the new Morgan sports car.

6. Answers may vary. Some suggested words are: timeless, reinvigorated, agile, faster, emotionally sensational, stunning, outstanding, unparalleled.

References to the effects these words may have on the reader, may refer to: building suspense, developing empathy, appealing to the senses, exciting interest, making the Morgan stand out and increasing the car's appeal.

7. Possible definitions are:

(a) *reinvigorated*: given new strength or energy

(b) *sensational*: causing great interest and excitement; thrilling

(c) *successor*: a person or thing that succeeds, or follows, another; the next model

(d) *exclusivity*: individuality; uniqueness; being part of an elite club

Exercise 8.4

1. a piece of cake – *easy to do, requiring little or no effort*
2. on thin ice – *in dangerous or troublesome territory; concerning a controversial subject*
3. barking up the wrong tree – *to accuse or blame the wrong person*
4. heads will roll! – *someone will be in trouble for this; the person(s)responsible will be punished*
5. to turn over a new leaf – *to begin afresh; to start anew; to make more effort this time*
6. to see eye to eye – *to be in agreement with someone (in general)*
7. to lose face – *to be humiliated / embarrassed*
8. to keep an eye on something – *to watch over something*
9. the lion's share – *the biggest part; more than one's fair share; almost everything*
10. to have other fish to fry – *to have other, more important things to do / think about*

Exercise 8.5

Answers may vary. Some suggested translations are:

2. The investigators soon managed to get to the heart of the problem.
   The investigators were soon able to identify the main source of the problem.
3. The children made a bee-line for the sweet shop.
   The children made a quick dash for the sweet shop.
4. After suffering a cold, Michelle was left with a frog in her throat.
   After suffering a cold, Michelle was left with a croaky voice.
5. Mr Simmons was forced to sell the house, lock, stock and barrel.
   Mr Simmons was forced to sell the house and all its contents.
6. The plan was going well until Michael threw a spanner in the works.
   The plan was going well until Michael spoiled it.

7. On the day of the results, the students were on tenterhooks.
    On the day of the results, the students were feeling very nervous.
8. When Jane returned from Guide camp, she slept like a log.
    When Jane returned from Guide camp, she slept well.
9. 'I like to call a spade a spade,' said Grandad.
    'I like to speak plainly,' said Grandad.
10. After months of arguing, the pair agreed to bury the hatchet.
    After months of arguing, the pair agreed to end their feud.

Exercise 8.6

1. <u>Relax</u> beneath the shade of a palm tree.
2. <u>Feel</u> the silky smooth sand between your toes and <u>hear</u> the waves lapping against the shore.
3. <u>Switch</u> into fifth gear, <u>accelerate</u> and <u>enjoy</u> the ride of your life.
4. Sunshine holidays: <u>let</u> your worries drift away.
5. <u>Call</u> your local showroom for details.

Exercise 8.7

Answers will vary. Some interesting synonyms are:

1. small – petite, miniature, tiny, diminutive
2. happy – blissful, elated, joyful, jubilant, thrilled
3. sad – dejected, depressed, melancholy, glum
4. scared – anxious, frightened, petrified, intimidated
5. old – decrepit, grizzled, senile, ancient, mature

Exercise 8.8

Answers will vary once again. Interesting examples are:

1. fast – brisk, nippy, hasty, rapid, hurried
2. nice – agreeable, delightful, amiable, commendable
3. loud – thunderous, blaring, ear-splitting, rowdy
4. lazy – indolent, slothful, idle, languid
5. charming – bewitching, appealing, delectable, charismatic

Exercise 8.9

Answers will vary. Some suggested words are:

1. Is that *correct / true / accurate*?
2. I'm *delighted / relieved / pleased* to hear it.
3. The prisoner has been accused of *seizing / snatching / stealing* and driving away a motor car.
4. Oh that's very *thoughtful / compassionate / considerate* of you...
5. With one small *condition / provision / stipulation*...

Chapter 9

Exercise 9.1

1. The joy of stumbling across an earwig's nest was especially overwhelming for Gerald because he had wanted to find one for a long time and had searched everywhere without success.

2. (a) The insect was struck by a flood of sunlight as Gerald lifted the bark.
   (b) The insect did not move when the sunlight hit her.

3. Answers may vary, eg:
   This tells us that Gerald's love of plants and animals was so strong, he was able to spell their names perfectly – because he had seen them written down and was very familiar with them. He was able to spell the words and phrases that interested him.

4. Answers may vary, eg:
   Gerald had seen the earwig when it was a baby, being nursed by its mother. He would have liked to think that the insect was saluting him now – remembering him from their last meeting – but he knew this was more likely to be a warning to stay away.

5. The baby earwig raised his pincers as a warning signal to stay away.

6. Acceptable words and phrases include: 'exciting discovery'; 'I had long wanted to find one'; 'like suddenly being given a present'; 'it was a heart-warming sight'.

7. Possible definitions are:
   (a) *complement*: something making up a whole (noun); to add to/complete something (verb)
   (b) *tenderly*: gently; delicately
   (c) *scrutiny*: close examination; investigation
   (d) *brood*: family of young

Exercise 9.2

1. Earwigs like to hide under the bark of a tree or under stones.

2. Earwigs may have got their name because some of them have wings shaped like ears – and the name 'earwings' was changed to 'earwigs'.

3. Earwigs use their pincers to defend themselves and in courtship displays.

4. You can tell the difference between male and female earwigs by looking at their pincers. Male earwigs have rounded pincers, while females have straighter ones.

5. Earwig mothers always stay and guard their eggs, tidying and cleaning them to remove any dirt or fungi, and protecting them from other insects or foraging birds. This shows they are good parents.

6. When they are born, earwigs are almost see-through, but their bodies darken as they get older. Young earwigs shed their skin up to five times before they are fully grown.

7. Acceptable definitions include:

(a). *pincers*: claws (or tools) for gripping

(b). *species*: sort; kind (especially animals)

(c). *nocturnal*: active at night (rather than at day)

(d). *moult*: cast or shed fur or feathers

Exercise 9.4

1. Look! I have found a nest of earwigs.
2. If I were an earwig I would not like my nest being disturbed.
3. Will you not come with me? You will enjoy seeing the nest.
4. I would rather be an ant than an earwig.
5. Earwigs like to eat plants but they will eat other insects too, if they get the chance.

Exercise 9.5

2. I have – I've
3. will not – won't
4. cannot – can't
5. do not – don't
6. we are – we're

Exercise 9.6

2. The whiskers belonging to the cat – *the cat's whiskers*
3. The truncheon belonging to the policeman – *the policeman's truncheon*
4. The bag belonging to the postman – *the postman's bag*
5. The nest belonging to the bird – *the bird's nest*

Exercise 9.7

2. The mother of Miss Atkins – *Miss Atkins's mother*
3. The pencil of Lucas – *Lucas's pencil*
4. The food of the penguins – *the penguins' food*
5. The church of St Thomas – *St Thomas's church*
6. The locker room of the players – *the players' locker room*

Exercise 9.8

2.	ungrateful – *grateful*
3.	happy – *unhappy*
4.	unlucky – *lucky*
5.	hopeless – *hopeful*
6.	legal – *illegal*
7.	incomplete – *complete*
8.	merciful – *merciless*
9.	convenient – *inconvenient*
10.	honest – *dishonest*

Chapter 10

Exercise 10.1

1. The river is referred to as the River Sea because it is very wide in places – almost as wide as a sea.
2. Maia thought the alligator was a log because it looked so similar – grey and motionless.
3. The houses were built on stilts to prevent them from being flooded when the river rose.
4. The animals that receive a mention in the passage are: capybaras, parakeets, an alligator and dogs.
5. Answers may vary. Use the following as a guide:
   I think the Indian children were pleased to see Maia because they 'came out onto the landing stage and waved and called out' at her as she sailed past.
6. The different colours mentioned in the passage are: scarlet, blue and grey.
7. Possible definitions are:
   (a) *litter*: a brood of young born
   (b) *lumbered*: moved heavily or clumsily; rumbled
   (c) *verandas*: roofed galleries or terraces
8. Answers will vary. Look for references to key evidence from the passage, including: 'The journey down the Amazon was one that Maia never forgot'; 'they saw some of the creatures that Maia had read about' (which Maia would have enjoyed); 'Maia waved back and didn't stop till they were out of sight' (suggesting that Maia was happy to see them).

Exercise 10.2

1. Michael's cheekbone is swollen due to overexposure to the hot sun when he was reading on deck the day before.
2. Answers will vary; some suggestions are: as smooth and shiny as a mirror; untouched like freshly fallen snow.
3. The faint breeze has a very positive impact on Michael. He delights in it, describing it as 'voluptuously soft' like 'deliciousness itself'.
4. The 'enchantment' lasts for only a moment because the hot sun reappears overhead, warming the land and turning the air humid again.
5. Answers may vary; a suggested answer follows:
   When Michael first rises, he feels 'grotty and puffy', suffering from the effects of sunstroke from the previous day. He has to walk barefooted through 'greasy oil and the remains of smoked fish'. Gradually, the 'mother-of-pearl' river and the beautiful sky

cheer his mood and he soon breathes in 'deliciousness itself', as the faint breeze cools him. However, this refreshing (and refreshed) mood lasts only a moment, as the sun soon reappears and 'the heat of the day begins'.

6.   The colours referred to in the passage are: white, purple, ultramarine, pink and pale-red.
7.   (a) rise – verb
      (b) yesterday – noun
      (c) deliciousness – noun
      (d) greasy – adjective

Exercise 10.4

1.   When Michael woke up, <u>he</u> felt tired and poorly. (3)
2.   When Maia saw the alligator, <u>she</u> thought it was a log floating in the water. (3)
3.   The Indian children waved when <u>they</u> saw Maia going past. (3)
4.   I felt tired but <u>I</u> wasn't going to give up yet. (1)
5.   <u>I</u> could feel the oil and grease under my feet as I walked along the deck. (1)

Exercise 10.5

1.   In places the river was so wide that she <u>understood</u> why it was called the River Sea.
2.   The Indian children came out onto the landing stage and <u>waved</u>.
3.   The sun emerges from a belt of cloud and <u>bursts</u> out white-hot.
4.   The journey down the Amazon was one that Maia never <u>forgot</u>.
5.   It is five a.m. and I <u>feel</u> tired.

Exercise 10.6

We pass plantations of rubber trees and Indian villages with the houses built on stilts to stop them being flooded when the river rises. The Indian children come out onto the landing stage and wave and call out, and I wave back and don't stop till they are out of sight.
Sometimes the boat goes close enough to the shore for us to pass by old houses owned by the sugar planters or coffee exporters; we can see the verandas with the families taking tea, and dogs stretched out in the shade, and hanging baskets of scarlet flowers.

Exercise 10.8

1. accessory
2. opportunity
3. accommodation
4. excessive
5. impossible